The Art of Praying Scripture

The Art of Praying Scripture

Arla Mitchell

Come to the Fire Publishing
www.cometothefire.org

Table of Contents

Forward

I was a stay-at-home mom and intercessor, reading through the Bible each year as well as reading prayer books, practicing their methods of prayer many hours. Then I discovered a family member was into drugs. I was all prayed out, failed as a mother and intercessor.

One day, I prayed, "Lord, You are not being mean to me by not answering my prayers, but there must be skills in prayer I do not know, and I don't think anyone knows. I think these skills are hidden in the Word of God."

I started going to a church that teaches from Isaiah 62:6-7, "I have set a watchmen (intercessor) on thy walls O' Jerusalem, which will never hold their peace day nor night: Ye that make mention of the Lord, keep not silence, and give him no rest, until he establish, and till he make Jerusalem a praise in the earth."

I found Scripture for every need. My sorrow and grief caused me to walk the floor by the hour for over four years, reminding God of his promises.

One night, there was a knock on the bedroom door at 2:00 am. It was the child I had been praying for: "Mom and Dad, can I come in? I want to get my life right with the Lord." He went on to Bible College, teaching music when he graduated.

After that, I began receiving many answers to prayer from those Scriptures.

I went through another crisis with my husband's health. Then I learned a skill that would bring answers more quickly. Mark 11:24 says, "What things soever you desire, when you pray, believe that you receive them and ye shall have them." So I changed my prayers to thanking God that I now have the answer. God's joyful presence became mine as I agreed with God's word.

In 1995 at age 65, I wrote my story *Unlocking the Heavens* and then *Prayer Strategy Resource Book*. The "GO-YE" prayer pages activated a ministry sending me all over the world. The "Prosper" pages paid the way. (I have never asked for money.) The "Success" page made me succeed, and I am now published in a number of languages.

Arla Mitchell has written *The Art of Praying Scripture* using the same skills as *Prayer Strategy Resource Book* but using a number of other topics. I am sure her book will bring a harvest of answers to many.

Many of her topics have to do with developing our Christian character. In this time, God is calling His people. "If my people who are called by my name…." We are the ones to change. Now the Word of God which is full of power can go forth changing us from Glory to Glory. Yippee!!!

When Jesus died on the cross, He said, "It is finished." Now all the promises are Yea and Amen to us. All the blessings of heaven are now ours. So how do we receive the answers? We pray the Word rejoicing and agreeing that the answer is now ours. We look at the answer, not the problem. Then the Word of God, which is full of life, goes forth and brings God's plan for us.

In our day Americans are concerned, not only about our lives and families, but our country. People have been praying and fasting but are asking, "Where are the answers?" I think the Lord has brought forth these skills that activate the Word of God for us at this time in history.

Ruth Shinness, CEO of Prayer Strategy Ministries
www.prayerstrategy.org

Powerful Prayers

For years I hoped that one day I would learn how to pray. I had some vague notion that when I had become spiritually mature enough and perhaps had sprouted a few gray hairs, it would suddenly click, and I would become the prayer warrior of my dreams. Instead, I have been on a journey that has shown me I had it all backwards. Learning to pray is a lot like learning to ride a bike or bake a cheesecake. It takes practice. Lots of it.

That simple thought was so encouraging to me. I (and anyone else) could learn how to pray. I just had to be willing to put the time in, so to speak. We don't suddenly develop a desire to pray when we are spiritually mature; rather, maturity occurs as we are on our knees.

So, why don't more Christians delve into the world of prayer? After all, we have the privilege of communing with our Creator who longs to hear from us. As Charles Spurgeon said, "Prayer is the slender nerve that moveth the muscles of omnipotence."[1]

And consider the possible benefits of a rich prayer life: children growing up to love God, churches being unified, friends coming to know the One who died for them, marriages becoming richer and more Christ-like. The list keeps going.

Tapping into the Power Source

A number of years ago, my mom was talking to my cousin Ruth Ann. As Ruth Ann was flipping through her Bible, mom saw a list of names written on one of the back pages. When she asked about the names, Ruth Ann replied, "That's a list of the people I've led to the Lord in the last year."

"How many names are there?"

"Seventy," Ruth Ann answered.

How could one young woman see that many people pray to receive Christ in one year? Her secret was in praying Scripture, using the book *Prayer Strategies* by Ruth Shinness, combined with witnessing. My cousin had caught on to one of the most powerful tools we have as Christians—praying God's Word.

Mom immediately bought several of these books and gave me one. From that point on, my prayer life began to change as I incorporated Scripture into my regular prayer time.

George Mueller, known for his deep prayer life and faith in God, said when he was ninety, "I have never had an unanswered prayer." He said the secret to receiving answers lies in how we apply God's Word during prayer. He prayed with an open Bible and wouldn't voice a petition without a "word from God" to back that petition.[2]

Our own words are weak, and we often don't know how we should pray. That's why it's important that we pray His Words; they are powerful.

Praying with Faith

Charles Spurgeon stated, "Every promise of Scripture is a writing of God, which may be pleaded before Him with this reasonable request, 'Do as Thou hast said!' The Creator will not cheat the creature who depends upon His truth; and far more, the Heavenly Father will not break His word to His own child."[3]

Praying Scripture is a faith-builder. Psalm 138:2 says, "I praise your name for your unfailing love and faithfulness; for your promises are backed by all the honor of your name." (NLT) Imagine, God's honor is at stake! Since we know he always keeps his promises, why don't we pray with more faith?

Do we really believe Mark 11:24? "Therefore I tell you, whatever you ask for in prayer, believe that you have received it, and it will be yours." (NIV)

Most of the Scripture prayers in this book are written as faith statements. We can take God at his Word, and I have found that praying Scripture like I mean it increases my faith. "It is the same with my Word. I send it out, and it always produces fruit. It will accomplish all I want it to, and it will prosper everywhere I send it." (Isaiah 55:11 NLT)

If you find it hard to pray the Scriptures as faith statements, consider what Blaise Pascal, a 17th century French philosopher, told those struggling with their faith. He said they should act as though they believed; he considered that something as meager as acting as though they believed would qualify as the mustard seed of faith that Jesus promised would remove mountains.

For many years I lived with severe, even paralyzing, fear. God used Scripture to set me free, and I have found that one of the keys to remaining free is to pray his promises frequently. As I state his promises with confidence, my faith that he will do what he said continues to grow and the temptation to return to my anxious thoughts recedes.

When temptation or struggles come, ask God to lead you to a verse that applies to your situation. Then, when the enemy comes to spew lies into your ear, state with confidence God's Word. Let truth become the only thing you will listen to.

How to Use This Book

In this book, the prayer is in bold print, and the Scripture it is taken from is given directly underneath. As you pray these Scriptures, meditate on them and let God direct your prayers. It is also helpful to pray them out loud. We can declare with the author of Psalm 91: "I will say of the Lord..."

Also, you may notice that the topics are in alphabetical order with the exception of Worship and Repentance, which come first. Beginning our prayer time worshipping God reminds us of the powerful, awe-inspiring God we are bowing before and helps bring us into his presence. Then, it's important to pause in a time of confession to make sure there is no sin in our lives that might hinder our prayers. "If I had not confessed the sin in my heart, the Lord would not have listened." (Psalm 66:18 NLT)

One additional note: while these prayers are placed into categories, most of the Scriptures can be applied to many more circumstances, inserting different names and situations to meet those needs.

[1] Charles H. Spurgeon, *Twelve Sermons on Prayer* (Grand Rapids: Baker Book House, 1971), 31.

[2] Dick Eastman, *The Hour that Changes the World* (Grand Rapids: Chosen Books, 2002), 56.

[3] Ibid., pg. 56, 57.

Worship

Praise the Lord. Salvation and glory and power belong to you, our God. Your judgments are true and just.
After this, I heard what sounded like a vast crowd in heaven shouting, "Praise the Lord. Salvation and glory and power belong to our God. His judgments are true and just. (Revelation 19:1, 2a NLT)

Holy, holy, holy are you, Lord Almighty; the whole earth is full of your glory.
And they were calling to one another: "Holy, holy, holy is the Lord Almighty; the whole earth is full of his glory." (Isaiah 6:3 NIV)

It is good that I am giving thanks to you, Lord, and singing praises to your name, O Most High; I am declaring your lovingkindness in the morning and your faithfulness every night...For you, Lord, have made me glad through your work; I will triumph in the works of your hands.
It is good to give thanks to the Lord, and to sing praises to Your name, O Most High; To declare Your lovingkindness in the morning, And Your faithfulness every night...For You, Lord, have made me glad through Your work; I will triumph in the works of Your hands. (Psalm 92:1-2, 4 NKJV)

Our Lord and God, you are worthy to receive glory, honor and power. You created all things, and by your decisions they are and were created. Praise, honor, glory and strength forever and ever to you who sits on the throne and to the Lamb. Our God, who sits upon the throne, has the power to save his people, and so does the Lamb.

"Our Lord and God, you are worthy to receive glory, honor, and power. You created all things, and by your decision they are and were created." Then I heard all beings in heaven and on the earth and under the earth and in the sea offer praise. Together, all of them were saying, "Praise, honor, glory, and strength forever and ever to the one who sits on the throne and to the Lamb!" "Our God, who sits upon the throne, has the power to save his people, and so does the Lamb." (Revelation 4:11, 5:13, 7:10 CEV)

I give you the glory you deserve, O Lord, bringing you an offering and coming into your presence. I worship you in all your holy splendor.
Give to the Lord the glory he deserves! Bring your offering and come into his presence. Worship the Lord in all his holy splendor. (1 Chronicles 16:29 NLT)

O magnify the Lord with me, and let us exalt His name together.
O magnify the Lord with me, and let us exalt His name together. (Psalm 34:3 AMP)

Be exalted, O God, above the highest heavens! May your glory shine over all the earth.
Be exalted, O God, above the highest heavens! May your glory shine over all the earth. (Psalm 58:5 NLT)

I come in worship and bow down, kneeling before you, O Lord, my maker, for you are my God. I am one of the people you watch over, the flock under your care.
Come, let us worship and bow down. Let us kneel before the Lord our maker, for he is our God. We are the people he watches over, the flock under his care. (Psalm 95:6-7a NLT)

Repentance

I confess my sins to you, knowing that you are faithful and just to forgive my sins. You are cleansing me from from all unrighteousness.
If we confess our sins, He is faithful and just to forgive us *our* sins and to cleanse us from all unrighteousness. (I John 1:9 NKJV)

My spirit is contrite and humble, so you are living with me, O God. You restore my crushed spirit and also revive my courage because my heart is repentant.
The high and lofty one who lives in eternity, the Holy One, says this: "I live in the high and holy place with those whose spirits are contrite and humble. I restore the crushed spirit of the humble and revive the courage of those with repentant hearts. (Isaiah 57:15 NLT)

Thank you, O Lord, for being patient with me because you don't want me to perish; now I am repenting.
The Lord is not slow in keeping his promise, as some understand slowness. Instead he is patient with you, not wanting anyone to perish, but everyone to come to repentance. (2 Peter 3:9 NIV)

I am now obeying your command to repent.
Truly, these times of ignorance God overlooked, but now commands all men everywhere to repent. (Acts 17:30 NKJV)

I am not concealing my sins but am confessing and turning from them. That is why you are showing me mercy.
People who conceal their sins will not prosper, but if they confess and turn from them, they will receive mercy. (Proverbs 28:13 NLT)

I wandered away like a lost sheep; thank you for coming and finding me, for I have not forgotten your commands.
I have wandered away like a lost sheep; come and find me, for I have not forgotten your commands. (Psalm 119:176 NLT)

Thank you for sweeping away my sins like a cloud and scattering my offenses like the morning mist. I return to you, for you have paid the price to set me free.
I have swept away your sins like a cloud. I have scattered your offenses like the morning mist. Oh, return to me, for I have paid the price to set you free. (Isaiah 44:22 NLT)

I thank you, Father, that you do not desire a sacrifice or a burnt offering but a broken spirit. You are not rejecting my broken and repentant heart.
You do not desire a sacrifice, or I would offer one. You do not want a burnt offering. The sacrifice you desire is a broken spirit. You will not reject a broken and repentant heart, O God. (Psalm 51:16, 17 NLT)

I have repented and now there is joy in the presence of the angels of God.
I tell you, there is joy in the presence of the angels of God over one sinner who repents. (Luke 15:10 NASB)

Thank you for wiping the slate of all my wrongdoings. There's nothing left of my sins. I've come back to you and have been redeemed.
I've wiped the slate of all your wrongdoings. There's nothing left of your sins. Come back to me, come back. I've redeemed you. (Isaiah 44:22 The Message)

I am repenting so that I will not perish.
I tell you, no; but unless you repent you will all likewise perish. (Luke 13:3 NKJV)

Children

You, God, are changing my heart and the hearts of all my descendants, so that we love you with all our heart and soul and now we live!
The Lord your God will change your heart and the hearts of all your descendants, so that you will love him with all your heart and soul and so you may live! (Deuteronomy 30:6 NLT)

Thank you, God, for teaching my children; they now enjoy great peace.
I will teach all your children, and they will enjoy great peace. (Isaiah 54:13 NLT)

You are pouring your Spirit on my descendants, and your blessing on my offspring. They are springing up among the grass, like willows by the watercourses. They are saying, "I belong to the Lord."
I will pour My Spirit on your descendants, and My blessing on your offspring; they will spring up among the grass, like willows by the watercourses.' One will say, 'I am the Lord's'; another will call himself by the name of Jacob; another will write with his hand, 'The Lord's,' and name himself by the name of Israel. (Isaiah 44:3-5 NKJV)

My children are a gift from you, Lord; they are truly a blessing.
Children are a blessing and a gift from the Lord. (Psalm 127:3 CEV)

Thank you for letting us see you work again, for letting our children see your glory.
Let us, your servants, see you work again; let our children see your glory. (Psalm 90:16 NLT)

Thank you that my children are doing the right thing by obeying their parents. They are honoring their father and mother, so it is going well with them and they are enjoying a long life on the earth.
Children, obey your parents in the Lord, for this is right. "Honor your father and mother"--which is the first commandment with a promise"--so that it may go well with you and that you may enjoy long life on the earth. (Ephesians 6:1-3 NIV)

Thank you that my children are running from anything that stimulates youthful lusts. Instead, they now pursue righteous living, faithfulness, love and peace, enjoying the companionship of those who call on you, Lord, with pure hearts.
Run from anything that stimulates youthful lusts. Instead, pursue righteous living, faithfulness, love, and peace. Enjoy the companionship of those who call on the Lord with pure hearts. (2 Timothy 2:22 NLT)

My children are careful to live blameless lives. They lead lives of integrity in their own home and refuse to look at anything vile and vulgar. They have nothing to do with those who deal crookedly. These children reject perverse ideas and stay away from every evil, not tolerating people who slander their neighbors. They do not endure conceit and pride, but search for faithful people to be their companions.
I will be careful to live a blameless life--when will you come to help me? I will lead a life of integrity in my own home. I will refuse to look at anything vile and vulgar. I hate all who deal crookedly; I will have nothing to do with them. I will reject perverse ideas and stay away from every evil. I will not tolerate people who slander their neighbors. I will not endure conceit and pride. I will search for faithful people to be my companions. (Psalm 101:2-6a NLT)

My children are increasing in wisdom and stature, and in favor with you, God, and men.
And Jesus increased in wisdom and stature, and in favor with God and men. (Luke 2:52 NKJV)

You, God, are working in my children, giving them both the desire and the power to do what pleases you.
For God is working in you, giving you the desire and the power to do what pleases him. (Philippians 2:13 NLT)

Thank you that they are doing nothing wrong but follow your ways, Lord.
They do no wrong but follow his ways. (Psalm 119:3 NIV)

Discretion is protecting my children, and understanding is guarding them. Wisdom is saving them from the ways of wicked men and from those whose words are perverse.
Discretion will protect you, and understanding will guard you. Wisdom will save you from the ways of wicked men, from men whose words are perverse, who have left the straight paths to walk in dark ways, who delight in doing wrong and rejoice in the perverseness of evil. (Proverbs 2:11-14 NIV)

Thank you, Lord, for this covenant with our family: Your spirit is upon me, and your words, which you have put in my mouth, shall not depart from my mouth, nor from my children's mouths nor from the mouths of my children's children.
"As for Me," says the Lord, "this is My covenant with them: My Spirit who is upon you, and My words which I have put in your mouth, shall not depart from your mouth, nor from the mouth of your descendants, nor from the mouth of your descendants' descendants," says the Lord, "from this time and forevermore." (Isaiah 59:21 NKJV)

You, God, are giving my children an undivided heart and putting a new spirit in them. You are removing their heart of stone and giving them a heart of flesh, so they are following your decrees, careful to keep your laws. They belong to you, and you are their God.
I will give them an undivided heart and put a new spirit in them; I will remove from them their heart of stone and give them a heart of flesh. Then they will follow my decrees and be careful to keep my laws. They will be my people, and I will be their God. (Ezekiel 11:19-20 NIV)

Thank you for helping my children to mature in physical strength and increase in wisdom. Your grace rests upon them.
Jesus grew up, maturing in physical strength and increasing in wisdom, and the grace of God rested on Him. (Luke 2:40 The Voice)

When enemies attack any in our family, you, the Eternal One, defeat them for us. They come against us from one direction but scatter and flee chaotically in seven different directions.
When your enemies attack you, the Eternal will defeat them for you. They'll come against you from one direction, but scatter and flee chaotically from you in seven different directions. (Deuteronomy 28:7 The Voice)

Thank you for not leading my children into temptation but delivering them from evil.
Lead us not into temptation, but deliver us from evil. (Matthew 6:13 KJV).

My children now realize you love them with an everlasting love.
I have loved you with an everlasting love. (Jeremiah 31:3 NASB)

Church

Our church is now going and making disciples of all nations, baptizing them in the name of the Father and of the Son and of the Holy Spirit, and teaching them to obey everything that was commanded us. You, Lord, are with us every day until the end of this present age.
Jesus came near and spoke to them, "I've received all authority in heaven and on earth. Therefore, go and make disciples of all nations, baptizing them in the name of the Father and of the Son and of the Holy Spirit, teaching them to obey everything that I've commanded you. Look, I myself will be with you every day until the end of this present age." (Matthew 28:18-20 CEB)

Lord, you are faithful, giving our church strength and protecting us from the evil one.
But the Lord is faithful and will give you strength and protect you from the evil one. (2 Thessalonians 3:3 CEB)

In our church we are aiming for harmony, building each other up.
So then, let us aim for harmony in the church and try to build each other up. (Romans 14:19 NLT)

Our church is being strengthened in the faith and our numbers are flourishing.
So the churches were strengthened in the faith and every day their numbers flourished. (Acts 16:5 CEB)

You, God, began this good work within our church and will continue it until it is finally finished.
And I am certain that God, who began the good work within you, will continue his work until it is finally finished on the day when Christ Jesus returns. (Philippians 1:6 NLT)

Our church is not gaining possession of the land in our own strength, but by your right hand, your arm, and the light of your countenance, because you favor us.
For they did not gain possession of the land by their own sword, nor did their own arm save them; but it was your right hand, your arm, and the light of your countenance, because you favored them. (Psalm 44:3 NKJV)

People are coming into our church and repenting and turning to you, God, so that their sins are wiped out, and times of refreshing are coming from you.
Repent, then, and turn to God, so that your sins may be wiped out, that times of refreshing may come from the Lord (Acts 3:19 NIV)

Thank you, Father, that in our church we are conducting ourselves with all humility, gentleness, and patience. We now accept each other with love.
Conduct yourselves with all humility, gentleness, and patience. Accept each other with love. (Ephesians 4:2 CEB)

I praise you, Father, that you give us endurance and encouragement and the same same attitude toward each other that Christ Jesus had. Now with one mind and one voice we glorify you, the God and Father of our Lord Jesus Christ.
May the God who gives endurance and encouragement give you the same attitude of mind toward each other that Christ Jesus had, so that with one mind and one voice you may glorify the God and Father of our Lord Jesus Christ. (Romans 15:5, 6 NIV)

Together we magnify you, Oh Lord, and we exalt your name together!
Oh, magnify the LORD with me, and let us exalt his name together! (Psalm 34:3 ESV)

Discernment

Thank you for giving me understanding to keep your law and to obey it with all my heart.
Give me understanding, so that I may keep your law and obey it with all my heart. (Psalm 119:34 NIV)

Because you have given me wisdom and a discerning heart, I am acquiring knowledge, for my ears are seeking it out.
The heart of the discerning acquires knowledge, for the ears of the wise seek it out. (Proverb 18:15 NIV)

Instead of believing every spirit, I am testing them to see if they are from you, God, so I am not deceived by the many false prophets who are in the world.
Beloved, do not believe every spirit, but test the spirits to see whether they are from God, for many false prophets have gone out into the world. (I John 4:1 ESV)

I trust in you, Lord, with all my heart and don't lean on my own understanding. I submit to you in all my ways, so you are making my paths straight.
Trust in the Lord with all your heart and lean not on your own understanding; in all your ways submit to him, and he will make your paths straight. (Proverb 3:5, 6 NIV)

I accept your words and store your commands within me, turning my ear to wisdom and applying my heart to understanding. I call out for insight and cry aloud for understanding, searching for it as for silver or hidden treasure. Because I have done this, I will understand the fear of the Lord and find the knowledge of God.
My son, if you accept my words and store up my commands within you, turning your ear to wisdom and applying

24

your heart to understanding--indeed, if you call out for insight and cry aloud for understanding, and if you look for it as for silver and search for it as for hidden treasure, then you will understand the fear of the Lord and find the knowledge of God. (Proverb 2:1-5 NIV)

Thank you for helping me to understand the meaning of your commandments. I am meditating on your wonderful deeds.
Help me understand the meaning of your commandments, and I will meditate on your wonderful deeds. (Psalm 119:27 NLT)

You are giving me understanding and I am obeying your instructions; I am putting them into practice with all my heart.
Give me understanding and I will obey your instructions; I will put them into practice with all my heart. (Psalm 119:34 NLT)

I believe in your commands, so now you are teaching me good judgment and knowledge.
I believe in your commands; now teach me good judgment and knowledge. (Psalm 119:66 NLT)

Thank you, Father, for clearly showing me your will and for helping me to achieve the knowledge and insight that can only come from you.
Father, may they clearly know Your will and achieve the height and depth of spiritual wisdom and understanding. (Colossians 1:9 The Voice)

Your word is a lamp that gives light wherever I walk.
Your word is a lamp that gives light wherever I walk. (Psalm 119:105 CEV)

Fear

When I am afraid, I put my trust in you. I praise you, O God, for your promises. Because I trust in you, I am not afraid. What can mere mortals do to me?

But when I am afraid, I will put my trust in you. I praise God for what he has promised. I trust in God, so why should I be afraid? What can mere mortals do to me? (Psalm 56:3, 4 NLT)

I won't be afraid for you, Lord, are with me. What can anyone do to me?

The Lord is for me--I won't be afraid. What can anyone do to me? (Psalm 118:6 CEB)

I thank you, God, that you have not given me a spirit of fear and timidity. Instead, I have power, love and self discipline.

For God has not given us a spirit of fear and timidity, but of power, love, and self-discipline. (2 Timothy 1:7 NLT)

Rather than being afraid and panicking, I am strong and courageous. For you, God, are personally going ahead of me. You will neither fail nor abandon me.

So be strong and courageous! Do not be afraid and do not panic before them. For the Lord your God will personally go ahead of you. He will neither fail you nor abandon you. (Deuteronomy 31:6 NLT)

Because you are constantly my refuge and strength, I will not fear.

God is our refuge and strength, an ever-present help in trouble. Therefore we will not fear, though the earth give way and the mountains fall into the heart of the sea. (Psalm 46:1, 2 NIV)

I have nothing to fear, for you are with me. I don't look around in terror, feeling dismayed, for you are my God. You strengthen me and help, holding me up with your victorious right hand.
Fear not [there is nothing to fear], for I am with you; do not look around you in terror and be dismayed, for I am your God. I will strengthen and harden you to difficulties, yes, I will help you; yes, I will hold you up and retain you with my [victorious] right hand of rightness and justice. (Isaiah 41:10 AMP)

Whenever I am afraid, I will put my trust and reliance in you. With your help, I will praise your word, confidently putting my trust in you; I will not fear. What can any man do to me?
What time I am afraid, I will have confidence in and put my trust and reliance in you. By [the help of] God I will praise His word; on God I lean, rely, and confidently put my trust; I will not fear. What can man, who is flesh, do to me? (Psalm 56:3, 4 AMP)

Because I dwell in the shelter of the Most High, I rest in the shadow of the Almighty. I say of the Lord, "He is my refuge and my fortress, my God, in whom I trust."
Whoever dwells in the shelter of the Most High will rest in the shadow of the Almighty. I will say of the Lord, "He is my refuge and my fortress, my God, in whom I trust." (Psalm 91:1, 2 NIV)

I lie down and fall asleep in peace because you alone, Lord, let me live in safety.
I will lie down and fall asleep in peace because you alone, Lord, let me live in safety. (Psalm 4:8 CEB)

Fearing God

Thank you for giving me a heart that always fears you and helping me to obey all your commandments. Because of this, it is going well with me and with my children forever.
Oh, that they had such a heart in them that they would fear Me and always keep all My commandments, that it might be well with them and with their children forever! (Deuteronomy 5:29 NKJV)

Thank you for putting a new song of praise in my mouth. Now many people fear you and put their trust in you.
He put a new song in my mouth, a hymn of praise to our God. Many will see and fear the Lord and put their trust in him. (Psalm 40:3 NIV)

I fear you, God; you are the only one I serve.
Fear the Lord your God, serve him only and take your oaths in his name. (Deuteronomy 6:13 NIV)

But you, Lord, watch over me because I fear you and rely on your unfailing love.
But the Lord watches over those who fear him, those who rely on his unfailing love. (Psalm 33:18 NLT)

Because I fear you, Lord, you have given me true wisdom, and because I have forsaken evil, you have given me real understanding.
And this is what he says to all humanity: "The fear of the Lord is true wisdom; to forsake evil is real understanding." (Job 8:28 NLT)

I fear you and serve you faithfully with all my heart. I love to remember the great things you have done for me.

Just fear the Lord and serve him faithfully with all your heart. Look at what great things he has done for you! (I Samuel 12:24 CEB)

How great is the goodness you have stored up for me because I fear you. You lavish it on me as I come to you for protection, blessing me before the watching world.
How great is the goodness you have stored up for those who fear you. You lavish it on those who come to you for protection, blessing them before the watching world. (Psalm 31:19 NLT)

You are my secure fortress because I fear you. This will be a refuge for my children. You have given me a fountain of life.
Whoever fears the Lord has a secure fortress, and for their children it will be a refuge. The fear of the Lord is a fountain of life, turning a person from the snares of death. (Proverbs 14:26, 27 NIV)

Who won't fear you, Lord, and glorify your name? You alone are holy. All nations will come and fall down in worship before you, for your acts of justice have been revealed.
Who won't fear you, Lord, and glorify your name? You alone are holy. All nations will come and fall down in worship before you, for your acts of justice have been revealed. (Revelation 15:4 CEB)

Because I fear you, the angel of the Lord encamps all around me and delivers me.
The angel of the Lord encamps all around those who fear Him, and delivers them. (Psalm 34:7 NKJV)

Freedom

Because you have set me free, I am really free!
Therefore, if the Son makes you free, you really will be free. (John 8:36 NLT)

Thank you that I am free, but I am also God's slave, so I don't use my freedom as an excuse to do evil.
For you are free, yet you are God's slaves, so don't use your freedom as an excuse to do evil. (I Peter 2:16 NLT)

I know the truth, and it has set me free.
Then you will know the truth, and the truth will set you free. (John 8:32 NIV)

Christ, you have set me free, and so I stand firm, not going back into the bondage of slavery.
Christ has set us free for freedom. Therefore, stand firm and don't submit to the bondage of slavery again. (Galatians 5:1 CEB)

Thank you, Lord, that your Spirit is with me, and so I have freedom.
Now the Lord is the Spirit, and where the Spirit of the Lord is, there is freedom. (2 Corinthians 3:17 NIV)

Thank you that there is now no condemnation for me because I am in Christ Jesus and I am set free from the law of sin and death. Because God sent you, Jesus, I do not live according to the flesh but according to the Spirit.
Therefore, there is now no condemnation for those who are in Christ Jesus, because through Christ Jesus the law of the Spirit who gives life has set you free from the law of sin and death. For what the law was powerless to do because it was weakened by the flesh, God did by sending his own

Son in the likeness of sinful flesh to be a sin offering. And so he condemned sin in the flesh, in order that the righteous requirement of the law might be fully met in us, who do not live according to the flesh but according to the Spirit. (Romans 8:1-4 NIV)

Thank you that I have been set free from sin and have become a slave to right living.
And having been set free from sin, you became slaves of righteousness. (Romans 6:18 NKJV)

You have not made me timid but have given me power, love and self-discipline.
For the Spirit God gave us does not make us timid, but gives us power, love and self-discipline. (2 Timothy 1:7 NIV)

I praise you that when I am in distress, I call to you and you answer me, setting me free.
Out of my distress I called on the LORD; the LORD answered me and set me free. (Psalm 118:5 ESV)

Thank you that I have been called to freedom; I don't use this freedom to indulge my selfish impulses but to serve others through love.
You were called to freedom, brothers and sisters; only don't let this freedom be an opportunity to indulge your selfish impulses, but serve each other through love. (Galatians 5:13 CEB)

Now I have been set free from sin and am God's slave. This is making me holy and will lead to eternal life.
Now you have been set free from sin, and you are God's slaves. This will make you holy and will lead you to eternal life. (Romans 6:22 CEV)

Government

Our leaders' hearts are like streams of water directed by you, Lord; you guide them wherever you please.
The king's heart is like a stream of water directed by the Lord; he guides it wherever he pleases. (Proverbs 21:1 NLT)

Blessed are our leaders who trust in you, Lord, and have made you their hope and confidence. These men and women are like trees planted along a riverbank, with roots that reach deep into the water. They are not bothered by the heat or worried by long months of drought. Their leaves stay green, and they never stop producing fruit.
But blessed are those who trust in the Lord and have made the Lord their hope and confidence. They are like trees planted along a riverbank, with roots that reach deep into the water. Such trees are not bothered by the heat or worried by long months of drought. Their leaves stay green, and they never stop producing fruit. (Jeremiah 17:7, 8 NLT)

Thank you that our leaders accept divine guidance. Because they obey your law, they are joyful.
When people do not accept divine guidance, they run wild. But whoever obeys the law is joyful. (Proverbs 29:18 NLT)

Thank you for removing the moral rot within our nation. We now have wise and knowledgeable leaders, which is bringing stability.
When there is moral rot within a nation, its government topples easily. But wise and knowledgeable leaders bring stability. (Proverbs 28:2 NLT)

Our president detests wrongdoing, for his rule is built on justice.
A king detests wrongdoing, for his rule is built on justice. (Proverbs 16:12 NLT)

I pray for our president and all those in authority, that they rule in such a way that we may live peaceful and quiet lives in all godliness and holiness.
I urge, then, first of all, that petitions, prayers, intercession and thanksgiving be made for all people--for kings and all those in authority, that we may live peaceful and quiet lives in all godliness and holiness. (I Timothy 2:1-3 NIV)

Thank you that we can rejoice because righteous men and women are in authority.
When the righteous are in authority, the people rejoice; but when a wicked man rules, the people groan. (Proverbs 29:2 NKJV)

Our president is just, providing stability for our nation. He does not demand bribes.
A just king gives stability to his nation, but one who demands bribes destroys it. (Proverbs 29:4 NLT)

I thank you that our leaders are filled with the knowledge of your will in all spiritual wisdom and understanding. They walk in a manner worthy of you, Lord, fully pleasing to you, bearing fruit in every good work and increasing in the knowledge of God.
We have not ceased to pray for you, asking that you may be filled with the knowledge of his will in all spiritual wisdom and understanding, so as to walk in a manner worthy of the Lord, fully pleasing to him, bearing fruit in every good work and increasing in the knowledge of God. (Colossians 1:9-10 ESV)

Our leaders are turning from their sins and now have new hearts and new spirits. They are changing their ways.
This is what the Lord God says. Turn, turn away from all your sins. Don't let them be sinful obstacles for you. Abandon all of your repeated sins. Make yourselves a new heart and a new spirit. Why should you die, house of Israel? I most certainly don't want anyone to die! This is what the Lord God says. Change your ways, and live! (Ezekiel 18:30b-32 CEB)

I praise you, God, for wisdom and might are yours. You change the times and the seasons. You remove kings and raise up kings. You give wisdom and knowledge to our leaders.
Blessed be the name of God forever and ever, For wisdom and might are His. And He changes the times and the seasons; He removes kings and raises up kings; He gives wisdom to the wise and knowledge to those who have understanding. (Daniel 2:20, 21 NKJV)

I praise you, Jesus, because the government of my country is on your shoulder. Your name is Wonderful Counselor, Mighty God, Everlasting Father, Prince of Peace.
For to us a child is born, to us a son is given; and the government shall be upon his shoulder, and his name shall be called Wonderful Counselor, Mighty God, Everlasting Father, Prince of Peace. (Isaiah 9:6 NIV)

Thank you for a president who judges the poor with truth.
If a king judges the poor with truth, His throne will be established forever. (Proverbs 29:14 NASB)

Harmony

We are making every effort to keep ourselves united in the Spirit, binding ourselves together with peace.
Make every effort to keep yourselves united in the Spirit, binding yourselves together with peace. (Ephesians 4:3 NLT)

You are helping us to agree with one another in what we say so there are no divisions among us. Rather, we are perfectly united in mind and thought.
I appeal to you, brothers and sisters, in the name of our Lord Jesus Christ, that all of you agree with one another in what you say and that there be no divisions among you, but that you be perfectly united in mind and thought. (I Corinthians 1:10 NIV)

Thank you that we are agreeing wholeheartedly with each other, loving one another and working together with one mind and purpose.
Then make me truly happy by agreeing wholeheartedly with each other, loving one another, and working together with one mind and purpose. (Philippians 2:2 NLT)

We are all like-minded and sympathetic to each other. We love one another, being compassionate and humble.
Finally, all of you, be like-minded, be sympathetic, love one another, be compassionate and humble. (I Peter 3:8 NIV)

We clothe ourselves with love, which binds us together in perfect harmony.
Above all, clothe yourselves with love, which binds us all together in perfect harmony. (Colossians 3:14 NLT)

We are joyful and growing to maturity, encouraging each other and living in harmony and peace. This is why you, the God of love and peace, are with us.
Dear brothers and sisters, I close my letter with these last words: Be joyful. Grow to maturity. Encourage each other. Live in harmony and peace. Then the God of love and peace will be with you. (2 Corinthians 13:11 NLT)

How good and pleasant it is that we are dwelling together in unity.
Behold, how good and how pleasant it is for brethren to dwell together in unity! (Psalm 133:1 AMP)

You, God, give us patience and encouragement, helping us live in complete harmony with each other, as is fitting for followers of Christ Jesus. We all join together with one voice, giving praise and glory to you. We accept each other just as Christ accepted us so that you receive glory.
May God, who gives this patience and encouragement, help you live in complete harmony with each other, as is fitting for followers of Christ Jesus. Then all of you can join together with one voice, giving praise and glory to God, the Father of our Lord Jesus Christ. Therefore, accept each other just as Christ has accepted you so that God will be given glory. (Romans 15:5-7 NLT)

You are helping us live in harmony with each other; we are not haughty but readily adjust ourselves to other people and are willing to perform humble tasks. We don't overestimate ourselves.
Live in harmony with one another; do not be haughty (snobbish, high-minded, exclusive), but readily adjust yourself to [people, things] and give yourselves to humble tasks. Never overestimate yourself or be wise in your own conceits. (Romans 12:16 AMP)

Healing

You, Lord, care for me when I am sick and restore me to health.
The Lord nurses them when they are sick and restores them to health. (Psalm 41:3 NLT)

Thank you that all is well with me and that I enjoy good health as I am prospering spiritually.
Dear friend, I'm praying that all is well with you and that you enjoy good health in the same way that you prosper spiritually. (3 John 1:2 CEB)

You have healed me and revealed to me an abundance of peace and truth.
Behold, I will bring it health and healing; I will heal them and reveal to them the abundance of peace and truth. (Jeremiah 33:6 NKJV)

My whole being blesses you, Lord, and I will never forget your good deeds: you have forgiven all my sins, healed all my sickness, saved my life and crowned me with faithful love and compassion.
Let my whole being bless the Lord and never forget all his good deeds: how God forgives all your sins, heals all your sickness, saves your life from the pit, crowns you with faithful love and compassion. (Psalm 103:2-4 CEB)

Heal me, O Lord, and I shall be healed; save me, and I shall be saved, for you are the One I praise.
Heal me, O Lord, and I shall be healed; save me, and I shall be saved, for You are my praise. (Jeremiah 17:14 AMP)

You have given me authority to cast out unclean spirits and to heal every disease and every sickness.

He called his twelve disciples and gave them authority over unclean spirits to throw them out and to heal every disease and every sickness. (Matthew 10:1 CEB)

My happy heart is doing me good, like medicine.
A merry heart does good, like medicine, but a broken spirit dries the bones. (Proverbs 17:22 NKJV)

I heal the sick and tell them, "The kingdom of God has come near to you."
Heal the sick who are there and tell them, "The kingdom of God has come near to you." (Luke 10:9 NIV)

You sent out your word and healed me, snatching me from the door of death.
He sent out his word and healed them, snatching them from the door of death. (Psalm 107:20 NLT)

You are instructing and teaching my doctors in the way they should go; you guide them with your eye.
I will instruct you and teach you in the way you should go; I will guide you with My eye. (Psalm 32:8 NKJV)

Thank you, Jesus, that my faith in you makes me well.
You heal me and give me peace.
And He said to her, "Daughter, your faith has made you well. Go in peace, and be healed of your affliction." (Mark 5:34 NKJV)

Holy Living

I belong to you, Christ Jesus, and have nailed the passions and desires of my sinful nature to your cross and crucified them there. Since I am living by the Spirit, I follow the Spirit's leading in every part of my life. **Thank you that I am not becoming conceited, provoking others, or being jealous of other people.**

Those who belong to Christ Jesus have nailed the passions and desires of their sinful nature to his cross and crucified them there. Since we are living by the Spirit, let us follow the Spirit's leading in every part of our lives. Let us not become conceited, or provoke one another, or be jealous of one another. (Galatians 5:24-26 NLT)

Thank you that as your obedient child I do not conform to evil desires. God, you are holy and are helping me to be holy.

As obedient children, do not conform to the evil desires you had when you lived in ignorance. But just as he who called you is holy, so be holy in all you do; for it is written: "Be holy, because I am holy." (I Peter 1:14-16 NIV)

These are the things I am thinking about—whatever is true, noble, right, pure, lovely and admirable—anything that is excellent or praiseworthy.

Finally, brothers and sisters, whatever is true, whatever is noble, whatever is right, whatever is pure, whatever is lovely, whatever is admirable—if anything is excellent or praiseworthy—think about such things. (Philippians 4:8 NIV)

Thank you that I may worship in your sanctuary and enter your presence on your holy hill because I lead a blameless life and do what is right, speaking the truth

from a sincere heart. I refuse to gossip, harm my neighbors or speak evil of my friends. I also despise flagrant sinners, honor the faithful followers of the Lord and keep my promises even when it hurts. I lend money without charging interest and cannot be bribed to lie about the innocent. Because of this, I will stand firm forever.

Who may worship in your sanctuary, Lord? Who may enter your presence on your holy hill? Those who lead blameless lives and do what is right, speaking the truth from sincere hearts. Those who refuse to gossip or harm their neighbor, or speak evil of their friends. Those who despise flagrant sinners, and honor the faithful followers of the Lord, and keep their promises even when it hurts. Those who lend money without charging interest, and who cannot be bribed to lie about the innocent. Such people will stand firm forever. (Psalm 15 NLT)

You, God, did not call me to be impure but are helping me to live a holy life.
For God did not call us to be impure, but to live a holy life. (I Thessalonians 4:7 NIV)

Thank you that I am holy because you, Lord, are holy. You have set me apart to be your very own.
You must be holy because I, the Lord, am holy. I have set you apart from all other people to be my very own. (Leviticus 20:26 NLT)

You, the God of peace, cause me to be completely dedicated to you, and my spirit, soul and body are being kept blameless until the Lord's coming.
Now, may the God of peace himself cause you to be completely dedicated to him; and may your spirit, soul, and body be kept intact and blameless at our Lord Jesus Christ's coming. (I Thessalonians 5:23 CEB)

Because I am born of God, I have overcome the world. This victory has been achieved through faith. For everyone born of God overcomes the world. This is the victory that has overcome the world, even our faith. (I John 5:4 NIV)

I have kept your ways, Lord; I am not guilty of turning away from you. All your laws are before me; I have not turned away from your decrees. I have been blameless before you and have kept myself from sin. For I have kept the ways of the Lord; I am not guilty of turning from my God. All his laws are before me; I have not turned away from his decrees. I have been blameless before him and have kept myself from sin. (Psalm 18:21-23 NIV)

I give you glory, God, for you equip me with everything good for doing your will, and you work in me what is pleasing to you through Jesus Christ. Now may the God of peace, who through the blood of the eternal covenant brought back from the dead our Lord Jesus, that great Shepherd of the sheep, equip you with everything good for doing his will, and may he work in us what is pleasing to him, through Jesus Christ to whom be glory for ever and ever. Amen. (Hebrews 13:20, 21 ESV)

Thank you for cleansing me from everything that defiles my body and spirit. I am working toward complete holiness because I fear you, God. Because we have these promises, dear friends, let us cleanse ourselves from everything that can defile our body or spirit. And let us work toward complete holiness because we fear God. (2 Corinthians 7:1 NLT)

Humility

Thank you, God, for giving me grace to stand against evil desires. You oppose the proud but favor me because I am humble.
But he gives us even more grace to stand against such evil desires. As the Scriptures say, "God opposes the proud but favors the humble." (James 4:6 NLT)

Thank you that I am obtaining wisdom because of my humble spirit.
When pride comes, then comes disgrace, but with humility comes wisdom. (Proverbs 11:2 NIV)

Because I am humble, you lead me in what is right and teach me your way.
He leads the humble in what is right, and the humble He teaches His way. (Psalm 25:9 AMP)

You have given me your love, God, which is patient and kind. I am not jealous, arrogant or boastful.
Love is patient, love is kind, it isn't jealous, it doesn't brag, it isn't arrogant. (I Corinthians 13:4 CEB)

You, Jesus, are giving me your attitude, so I am not selfish or trying to impress others. Instead, I am humble, thinking of others as better than myself and taking an interest in them.
Don't be selfish; don't try to impress others. Be humble, thinking of others as better than yourselves. Don't look out only for your own interests, but take an interest in others, too. You must have the same attitude that Christ Jesus had. (Philippians 2:3-5 NLT)

I don't think more highly of myself than I ought but use sober judgment, in accordance with the faith you, God, have given me.

For by the grace given me I say to every one of you: Do not think of yourself more highly than you ought, but rather think of yourself with sober judgment, in accordance with the faith God has distributed to each of you. (Romans 12:3 NIV)

God, you have shown me what is good and are helping me to do what you require: to do what is just, to love mercy and to walk humbly with you.

He has shown you, O man, what is good; and what does the Lord require of you but to do justly, to love mercy, and to walk humbly with your God? (Micah 6:8 NKJV)

No matter what I am doing, whether eating or drinking, or whatever I do, it is all for your honor and glory.

So then, whether you eat or drink, or whatever you may do, do all for the honor and glory of God. (I Corinthians 10:31 AMP)

Thank you that instead of trying to promote myself, I am receiving your approval because you, Lord, commend me.

It isn't the person who promotes himself or herself who is approved but the person whom the Lord commends. (2 Corinthians 10:18 CEB)

Rather than thinking my way is always right, I am willing to listen to counsel, which makes me wise.

The way of a fool is right in his own eyes, but he who listens to counsel is wise. (Proverbs 12:15 AMP)

Thank you, Father, for allowing me to live according to the Holy Spirit's leading in every part of my life. Because

I am following you, I am not conceited, irritated or jealous of others.
If we are living now by the Holy Spirit, let us follow the Holy Spirit's leading in every part of our lives. Let us not become conceited, or irritate one another, or be jealous of one another. (Galatians 5:25, 26 NLT).

Thank you for removing my haughty eyes, proud heart and evil actions, for these are all sin.
Haughty eyes, a proud heart, and evil actions are all sin. (Proverbs 21:4 NLT)

Because you love me and have chosen me as your own, I am gentle, kind, humble, meek and patient.
God loves you and has chosen you as his own special people. So be gentle, kind, humble, meek, and patient. (Colossians 3:12 CEV)

Thank you, God, for rescuing me because I am lowly.
When they're humbled, you will say: "Cheer up; God will rescue the lowly. (Job 22:29 CEB)

You are pleased with me because I am yours, and you give victory to me because I am humble.
The Lord is pleased with his people, and he gives victory to those who are humble. (Psalm 149: CEV)

Husband

We are honoring our marriage and staying faithful to each other.
Give honor to marriage, and remain faithful to one another in marriage. God will surely judge people who are immoral and those who commit adultery. (Hebrews 13:4 NLT)

Thank you that I have received favor from you, Lord, through my wife, and she is my treasure.
The man who finds a wife finds a treasure, and he receives favor from the Lord. (Proverbs 18:22 NLT)

I love my wife sacrificially, just as you, Christ, loved the church.
As for husbands, love your wives just like Christ loved the church and gave himself for her. (Ephesians 5:25 CEB)

Because we respect you, Christ, we submit to each other.
...and submit to each other out of respect for Christ. (Ephesians 5:21 CEB)

I love my wife and am not harsh, bitter or resentful toward her.
Husbands, love your wives [be affectionate and sympathetic with them] and do not be harsh *or* bitter *or* resentful toward them. (Colossians 3:19 AMP)

Thank you that I love my wife as much as I love myself.
So husbands ought to love their own wives as their own bodies; he who loves his wife loves himself. (Ephesians 5:28 NKJV)

I honor my wife, treating her with understanding so that my prayers will not be hindered.

In the same way, you husbands must give honor to your wives. Treat your wife with understanding as you live together...Treat her as you should so your prayers will not be hindered. (I Peter 3:7 NLT)

Thank you that I am happy with the wife I married. I am attracted to her, and we are deeply in love.
Be happy with the wife you married when you were young. She is beautiful and graceful, just like a deer; you should be attracted to her and stay deeply in love. (Proverbs 5:18, 19 CEV)

I live happily with my wife all the days of my life.
Live happily with the woman you love through all the meaningless days of life that God has given you under the sun. (Ecclesiastes 9:9a NLT)

Thank you, Lord, for giving me an understanding wife.
...only the Lord can give an understanding wife. (Proverbs 19:14 NLT)

Loss/Grief

I praise you, God, who has comforted me in all my troubles so that I can comfort others with the comfort I have received from you.
Praise be to the God and Father of our Lord Jesus Christ, the Father of compassion and the God of all comfort, who comforts us in all our troubles, so that we can comfort those in any trouble with the comfort we ourselves receive from God. (2 Corinthians 1:3-4 NIV)

You heal me when I am brokenhearted and bind up my wounds, curing my pains and sorrows.
He heals the brokenhearted and binds up their wounds [curing their pains and their sorrows]. (Psalm 147:3 AMP)

I cast all of my cares, anxieties, worries and concerns on you once and for all, for I know you care for me affectionately and watch over me.
Casting the whole of your care [all your anxieties, all your worries, all your concerns, once and for all] on Him, for He cares for you affectionately and cares about you watchfully. (I Peter 5:7 AMP)

You are close to me when I am brokenhearted and save me when I am crushed in spirit.
The Lord is close to the brokenhearted and saves those who are crushed in spirit. (Psalm 34:18 NIV)

Even if my flesh and my heart fail, you, God, are my strength and portion forever.
My flesh and my heart may fail, but God is the strength of my heart and my portion forever. (Psalm 73:26 NIV)

Rather than be troubled, I choose to trust in you.

Don't be troubled. Trust in God. Trust also in me. (John 14:1 CEB)

But you, Lord, who created me says to not be afraid, for you have ransomed me; you have called me by name; I am yours. When I go through deep waters, you are with you. When I pass through rivers of difficulty, I do not drown! When I walk through the fire of oppression, I am not burned up—the flames do not consume me. For you are the Lord my God, my Savior, the Holy One of Israel. But now, O Jacob, listen to the Lord who created you. O Israel, the one who formed you says, "Do not be afraid, for I have ransomed you. I have called you by name; you are mine. When you go through deep waters, I will be with you. When you go through rivers of difficulty, you will not drown. When you walk through the fire of oppression, you will not be burned up; the flames will not consume you. For I am the Lord, your God, the Holy One of Israel, your Savior." (Isaiah 43:1-3b NIV)

Thank you that when I walk through valleys as dark as death, I am not afraid. You are with me, and your shepherd's rod makes me feel safe.
I may walk through valleys as dark as death, but I won't be afraid. You are with me, and your shepherd's rod makes me feel safe. (Psalm 23:4 CEV)

I thank you that your unfailing love is my comfort, just as you have promised.
May your unfailing love be my comfort, according to your promise to your servant. (Psalm 119:76 NIV)

Thank you for blessing me as I mourn by showing me your comfort.
God blesses those who mourn, for they will be comforted. (Matthew 5:4 NLT)

The Lost

Thank you that they are now confessing their sins, and you are faithful to forgive and cleanse them from everything they've done wrong.
But if we confess our sins, he is faithful and just to forgive us our sins and cleanse us from everything we've done wrong. (I John 1:9 CEB)

You, Lord, are putting your laws in their minds and writing them on their hearts. You are their God, and they belong to you. They know you, and you now forgive their wickedness, not remembering their sins any more.
This is the covenant I will establish with the people of Israel after that time, declares the Lord. I will put my laws in their minds and write them on their hearts. I will be their God, and they will be my people. No longer will they teach their neighbor, or say to one another, 'Know the Lord,' because they will all know me, from the least of them to the greatest. For I will forgive their wickedness and will remember their sins no more." (Hebrews 8:10-12 NIV)

Your blood, Christ, is cleansing their consciences from their sinful acts so they are serving the living God.
How much more, then, will the blood of Christ, who through the eternal Spirit offered himself unblemished to God, cleanse our consciences from acts that lead to death, so that we may serve the living God! (Hebrews 9:14 NIV)

They have been crucified with you, Christ, and it is no longer they who live, but you who lives in them. They now live by faith in the Son of God who died for them.
I have been crucified with Christ; it is no longer I who live, but Christ lives in me; and the life which I now live in the

flesh I live by faith in the Son of God, who loved me and gave Himself for me. (Galatians 2:20 NKJV)

You, God, are giving them an undivided heart and putting a new spirit in them. You are removing their heart of stone and giving them a heart of flesh, so they are following your decrees, careful to keep your laws. They belong to you, and you are their God.

I will give them an undivided heart and put a new spirit in them; I will remove from them their heart of stone and give them a heart of flesh. Then they will follow my decrees and be careful to keep my laws. They will be my people, and I will be their God. (Ezekiel 11:19-20 NIV)

They are confessing with their mouth that Jesus is Lord and believing in their heart that you, God, raised him from the dead, so they are now saved.

If you confess with your mouth that Jesus is Lord and believe in your heart that God raised him from the dead, you will be saved. For it is by believing in your heart that you are made right with God, and it is by confessing with your mouth that you are saved. (Romans 10:9, 10 NLT)

Their minds are no longer blinded by the god of this age. They now see the light of the gospel that displays your glory, Christ.

The god of this age has blinded the minds of unbelievers, so that they cannot see the light of the gospel that displays the glory of Christ, who is the image of God. (2 Corinthians 4:4 NIV)

They walk in the light, and your blood, Jesus, is cleansing them from all sin.

But if we walk in the light as He is in the light, we have fellowship with one another, and the blood of Jesus Christ His Son cleanses us from all sin. (I John 1:7 NKJV)

You, God, made Christ, who never sinned, to be the offering for their sin, so that they are now being made right with you through Christ.
For God made Christ, who never sinned, to be the offering for our sin, so that we could be made right with God through Christ. (2 Corinthians 5:21 NKJV)

As far as east is from west—that's how far you have removed their sins from them.
As far as east is from west—that's how far God has removed our sin from us. (Psalm 103:12 CEB)

They now belong to you, Christ, and have become a new person. Their old life is gone, and a new life has begun!
This means that anyone who belongs to Christ has become a new person. The old life is gone; a new life has begun! (2 Corinthians 5:17 NLT)

I thank you that you have now ended their bondage. You have broken the yoke of slavery and lifted it from their shoulders.
In that day the Lord will end the bondage of his people. He will break the yoke of slavery and lift it from their shoulders. (Isaiah 10:27 NLT)

Love

Thank you that I love others. This is how everyone will know I am your disciple.
A new command I give you: Love one another. As I have loved you, so you must love one another. By this everyone will know that you are my disciples, if you love one another. (John 13:34, 35 NIV)

Everything I do is done with love.
Let all that you do be done with love. (I Corinthians 16:14 NKJV)

I love my enemies and do good to them. When I lend to them, I don't expect anything back.
But love your enemies, do good to them, and lend to them without expecting to get anything back. (Luke 6:35a NIV)

I don't just say that I love others; I show it by my actions.
Dear children, let's not merely say that we love each other; let us show the truth by our actions. (I John 3:18 NLT)

Since I love you, God, I also love my brother and sister.
And he has given us this command: Anyone who loves God must also love their brother and sister. (I John 4:21 NIV)

I love others with genuine affection and take delight in honoring them.
Love each other with genuine affection, and take delight in honoring each other. (Romans 12:10 NLT)

I love you, Lord, with all my heart, soul and mind.
Jesus replied: "Love the Lord your God with all your heart and with all your soul and with all your mind." (Matthew 22:37 NIV)

You are helping me obey your commandment to love others as you have loved me.
This is My commandment, that you love one another as I have loved you. (John 15:12 NKJV)

You are always with me, Lord, and are a mighty savior. You delight in me with gladness and with your love calm all my fears. You rejoice over me with joyful songs.
For the Lord your God is living among you. He is a mighty savior. He will take delight in you with gladness. With his love, he will calm all your fears. He will rejoice over you with joyful songs. (Zephaniah 3:17 NLT)

You are giving me your love, which is patient and kind. I'm not jealous, boastful, arrogant, rude or irritable. I don't seek my own advantage, keep a record of complaints or become happy with injustice, but I am happy with the truth. This kind of love puts up with all things, trusts, hopes and endures.
Love is patient, love is kind, it isn't jealous, it doesn't brag, it isn't arrogant, it isn't rude, it doesn't seek its own advantage, it isn't irritable, it doesn't keep a record of complaints, it isn't happy with injustice, but it is happy with the truth. Love puts up with all things, trusts in all things, hopes for all things, endures all things. (I Corinthians 13:4-7 CEB)

I show my love for you, God, by obeying your commandments, and they are not hard to follow.
We show our love for God by obeying his commandments, and they are not hard to follow. (I John 5:3 CEV)

Men

Thank you that the words of my mouth and the meditations of my heart are pleasing to you, Lord.
Let the words of my mouth and the meditations of my heart be pleasing to you, Lord, my rock and my redeemer. (Psalm 19:14 CEB)

Thank you that I have self-control, am worthy of respect and live wisely. I have sound faith and am filled with love and patience.
Teach the older men to exercise self-control, to be worthy of respect, and to live wisely. They must have sound faith and be filled with love and patience. (Titus 2:2 NLT)

You are helping me to pray by lifting up holy hands, without anger or argument.
Therefore, I want men to pray everywhere by lifting up hands that are holy, without anger or argument. (I Timothy 2:8 CEB)

Because I am a man of God, I flee evil and pursue righteousness, godliness, faith, love, patience and gentleness.
But you, O man of God, flee these things and pursue righteousness, godliness, faith, love, patience, gentleness. (I Timothy 6:11 NKJV)

Thank you, Lord, that I am blessed because I fear you and find great delight in your commands.
Praise the Lord. Blessed are those who fear the Lord, who find great delight in his commands. (Psalm 112:1 NIV)

I am a man who shows mercy, and so I am doing my own soul good.

The merciful man does good for his own soul, but he who is cruel troubles his own flesh. (Proverbs 11:17 NKJV)

Thank you for creating a clean heart in me, God; you are putting a new, faithful spirit deep inside me!
Create a clean heart for me, God; put a new, faithful spirit deep inside me! (Psalm 51:10 CEB)

Thank you that I am blessed because I do not walk with the wicked, stand in the path of sinners or sit in the company of mockers. Instead, my delight is in your law, Lord, and I meditate on it day and night. That is why I'm like a tree planted by streams of water, which yields its fruit in season and whose leaf does not wither--whatever I do prospers.
Blessed is the one who does not walk in step with the wicked or stand in the way that sinners take or sit in the company of mockers, but whose delight is in the law of the Lord, and who meditates on his law day and night. That person is like a tree planted by streams of water, which yields its fruit in season and whose leaf does not wither-- whatever they do prospers. (Psalm 1:1-3 NIV)

I am choosing to make wise friends so that I become more wise, rather than hurting myself by going around with fools.
Wise friends make you wise, but you hurt yourself by going around with fools. (Proverbs 13:20 CEV)

I thank you, Lord, that your wonderful kindness and understanding help me to keep on growing.
Let the wonderful kindness and the understanding that come from our Lord and Savior Jesus Christ help you to keep on growing. Praise Jesus now and forever! Amen. (2 Peter 3:18 CEV)

Nation/City

Thank you for making our city strong. We are surrounded by your walls of salvation, opening the gates for the righteous and faithful to enter.
Our city is strong! We are surrounded by the walls of God's salvation. Open the gates to all who are righteous; allow the faithful to enter. (Isaiah 26:1b, 2 NLT)

We, who are called by your name, are humbling ourselves, praying, craving your face, and turning from our wicked ways, and you are now hearing from heaven, forgiving our sins and healing our land.
If My people, who are called by My name, shall humble themselves, pray, seek, crave, and require of necessity My face and turn from their wicked ways, then will I hear from heaven, forgive their sin, and heal their land. (2 Chronicles 7:14 AMP)

This nation is blessed because our God is the Lord.
Blessed is the nation whose God is the Lord, the people he chose for his inheritance. (Psalm 33:12 NIV)

Godliness is making our nation great; we are not being disgraced by sin.
Godliness makes a nation great, but sin is a disgrace to any people. (Proverbs 14:34 NLT)

Thank you that violence is no longer heard in our land, nor is ruin or destruction within our borders. Instead, we are called by the names Salvation and Peace.
No longer will violence be heard in your land, nor ruin or destruction within your borders, but you will call your walls Salvation and your gates Peace. (Isaiah 60:18 NIV)

The people of our city are confessing our sins, and you are faithful and just to forgive our sins and cleanse us from everything we've done wrong.
But if we confess our sins, he is faithful and just to forgive us our sins and cleanse us from everything we've done wrong. (I John 1:9 CEB)

Thank you for sending peace across our nation and satisfying us with the finest foods.
He sends peace across your nation and satisfies your hunger with the finest wheat. (Psalm 147:14 NLT)

You are bringing peace in our land, and we are able to sleep with no cause for fear.
I will give you peace in the land, and you will be able to sleep with no cause for fear. (Leviticus 26:6a NLT)

Our nation is turning from our evil, so you are relenting and not carrying out the harm you intended for us.
But if that nation I warned turns from its evil, then I'll relent and not carry out the harm I intended for it. (Jeremiah 18:8 CEB)

Parenting

You are giving me singleness of heart and action so that I will always fear you—it is now going well for me and my children.
I will give them singleness of heart and action, so that they will always fear me and that all will then go well for them and for their children after them. (Jeremiah 32:39 NIV)

Thank you, Lord, that I am not making my children angry by the way I treat them but am bringing them up with the discipline and instruction that comes from you.
Fathers, do not provoke your children to anger by the way you treat them. Rather, bring them up with the discipline and instruction that comes from the Lord. (Ephesians 6:4 NLT)

Thank you for helping me to direct my children onto the right path; when they are older, they will not leave it.
Direct your children onto the right path, and when they are older, they will not leave it. (Proverbs 22:6 NLT)

I am disciplining my children so they will become wise; now I am not disgraced by them.
To discipline a child produces wisdom, but a mother is disgraced by an undisciplined child. (Proverbs 29:15 NLT)

I am telling my children that you are the only God and teaching them to love you with all their heart, soul and strength. I teach them these truths diligently when we're at home, on the road, before bed and when we get up in the morning.
Hear, O Israel: The Lord our God, the Lord is one! You shall love the Lord your God with all your heart, with all your soul, and with all your strength...You shall teach them

diligently to your children, and shall talk of them when you sit in your house, when you walk by the way, when you lie down, and when you rise up. (Deuteronomy 6:4-7 NKJV)

Thank you that I am disciplining my children while there is hope; this way, I am not ruining their lives.
Discipline your children while there is hope. Otherwise you will ruin their lives. (Proverbs 119:18 NLT)

You, God, are returning my heart to my children and my children's hearts to me.
...and he will return parents' hearts to their children and children's hearts to their parents. (Malachi 4:6a The Voice)

When the enemy comes in like a flood against my family, your Spirit is lifting up a standard against him.
When the enemy comes in like a flood, the Spirit of the Lord will lift up a standard against him. (Isaiah 59:19 NKJV)

I am telling my children about your glorious deeds, Lord; so my children know you—even those not yet born—and they will someday teach their own children. Each generation will set its hope anew on you, not forgetting your glorious miracles and obeying your commands. They won't be like those who have been stubborn and rebellious, refusing to give their hearts to God.
We will tell the next generation about the glorious deeds of the Lord...He commanded our ancestors to teach them to their children, so the next generation might know them— even the children not yet born—and they in turn will teach their own children. So each generation should set its hope anew on God, not forgetting his glorious miracles and obeying his commands. Then they will not be like their ancestors--stubborn, rebellious, and unfaithful, refusing to give their hearts to God. (Psalm 78:4b-8 NLT)

Pastor

You are helping my pastor to keep watch over himself and all the flock which you have given him to oversee. He is shepherd of your church, which you bought with your own blood.

Keep watch over yourselves and all the flock of which the Holy Spirit has made you overseers. Be shepherds of the church of God, which he bought with his own blood. (Acts 20:28 NIV)

My pastor is caring for the flock that you, God, have entrusted to him. He watches over our congregation willingly, not grudgingly nor for what he will get out of it, but because he is eager to serve you.

Care for the flock that God has entrusted to you. Watch over it willingly, not grudgingly—not for what you will get out of it, but because you are eager to serve God. (I Peter 5:2 NLT)

My pastor is not domineering but is an example of Christian living to our congregation.

Not domineering [as arrogant, dictatorial, and overbearing persons] over those in your charge, but being examples (patterns and models of Christian living) to the flock (the congregation). (I Peter 5:3 AMP)

Thank you that my pastor is above reproach and is faithful to his wife. He has self-control, lives wisely and has a good reputation. He also enjoys having guests in his home and is able to teach. Our pastor is not violent or a heavy drinker but is gentle, avoiding quarrels and the love of money.

So an elder must be a man whose life is above reproach. He must be faithful to his wife. He must exercise self-control, live wisely, and have a good reputation. He must enjoy having guests in his home, and he must be able to teach. He must not be a heavy drinker or be violent. He must be gentle, not quarrelsome, and not love money. (I Timothy 3:2, 3 NLT)

You are helping my pastor manage his household well. His children are obedient with complete respect for their parents.
They should manage their own household well—they should see that their children are obedient with complete respect. (I Timothy 3:4 CEB)

Our pastor is holding fast to the Word of God that he was taught, so he is able to give instruction and encouragement in sound doctrine, convicting those who are in error.
He must hold fast to the sure and trustworthy Word of God as he was taught it, so that he may be able both to give stimulating instruction and encouragement in sound (wholesome) doctrine and to refute and convict those who contradict and oppose it [showing the wayward their error]. (Titus 1:9 AMP)

I am thankful that my pastor preaches the word, always ready to do it whether or not it is convenient. He corrects, confronts and encourages with patience and instruction.
Preach the word. Be ready to do it whether it is convenient or inconvenient. Correct, confront, and encourage with patience and instruction. (2 Timothy 4:2 CEB)

Your word is near my pastor. It is in his mouth and his heart. He preaches the word of faith.
But what does it say? "The word is near you, in your mouth and in your heart" (that is, the word of faith which we preach). (Romans 10:8 NKJV)

Peace

You are keeping me in perfect peace because I trust in you; all my thoughts are fixed on you.
You will keep in perfect peace all who trust in you, all whose thoughts are fixed on you! (Isaiah 26:3 NLT)

I am living at peace with everyone to the best of my ability.
If possible, to the best of your ability, live at peace with all people. (Romans 12:18 CEB)

Thank you, Lord, for granting me your peace at all times and in every circumstance and condition no matter what comes. You are with me.
Now may the Lord of peace Himself grant you His peace (the peace of His kingdom) at all times and in all ways [under all circumstances and conditions, whatever comes]. The Lord [be] with you all. (2 Thessalonians 3:16 AMP)

You are helping me to be a peacemaker, so I am called a child of God.
Blessed are the peacemakers, for they will be called children of God. (Matthew 5:9 NIV)

I am making every effort to live in peace with others and to be holy.
Make every effort to live in peace with everyone and to be holy; without holiness no one will see the Lord. (Hebrews 12:14 NIV)

Thank you, God, for filling me with joy and peace as I trust in you, so I now overflow with hope through the Holy Spirit's power.

May the God of hope fill you with all joy and peace as you trust in him, so that you may overflow with hope by the power of the Holy Spirit. (Romans 15:13 NIV)

Thank you that when I lie down, I am not afraid; my sleep is sweet.
When you lie down, you will not be afraid; when you lie down, your sleep will be sweet. (Proverbs 3:24 NIV)

Because I belong to you, I live in peace, feeling calm and secure.
You, the Lord's people, will live in peace, calm and secure. (Isaiah 32:18 AMP)

Instead of paying back evil with more evil, I am doing things in a way that earns the respect of others. Rather than taking revenge on people, you are helping me to treat them with kindness. In this way, I am conquering evil by doing good.
Never pay back evil with more evil. Do things in such a way that everyone can see you are honorable. Dear friends, never take revenge. Leave that to the righteous anger of God. For the Scriptures say, "I will take revenge; I will pay them back," says the Lord. Instead, "If your enemies are hungry, feed them. If they are thirsty, give them something to drink. In doing this, you will heap burning coals of shame on their heads." Don't let evil conquer you, but conquer evil by doing good. (Romans 12:17, 19-21 NLT)

Thank you, Lord, for giving strength to me; you are blessing me with peace.
The Lord will give [unyielding and impenetrable] strength to His people; the Lord will bless His people with peace. (Psalm 29:11 AMP)

Persecution

You, Lord, are giving me peace and confidence, even though I have tribulation and trials. I am filled with courage, for you have overcome the word, depriving it of power to harm me.

I have told you these things, so that in Me you may have [perfect] peace and confidence. In the world you have tribulation and trials and distress and frustration; but be of good cheer [take courage; be confident, certain, undaunted]! For I have overcome the world. [I have deprived it of power to harm you and have conquered it for you.] (John 16:33 AMP)

Thank you that I am blessed because people are persecuting me for doing right.

Blessed are those who are persecuted for righteousness' sake, for theirs is the kingdom of heaven. (Matthew 5:10 NKJV)

God, you are blessing me when people insult me, persecute me and say all kinds of evil things about me because I follow you. I am rejoicing and full of gladness, for I will have a great reward in heaven.

Blessed are you when people insult you, persecute you and falsely say all kinds of evil against you because of me. Rejoice and be glad, because great is your reward in heaven, for in the same way they persecuted the prophets who were before you. (Matthew 5:11, 12 NIV)

You are helping me to love my enemies, bless those who curse me, do good to those who hate me and pray for those who persecute me.

But I say to you, love your enemies, bless those who curse you, do good to those who hate you, and pray for those who spitefully use you and persecute you. (Matthew 5:44 NKJV)

I am keeping a clear conscience, so that those who speak maliciously against my good behavior in Christ are ashamed of their slander.
...keeping a clear conscience, so that those who speak maliciously against your good behavior in Christ may be ashamed of their slander. (I Peter 3:16 NIV)

Thank you that I am not surprised about the fiery trials that have come to test me. Instead, I rejoice as I share your suffering, Christ, for I have overwhelming joy when your glory is revealed.
Dear friends, don't be surprised about the fiery trials that have come among you to test you. These are not strange happenings. Instead, rejoice as you share Christ's suffering. You share his suffering now so that you may also have overwhelming joy when his glory is revealed. (I Peter 4:12, 13 CEB)

Thank you that when I am mocked because of your name, I am blessed, for the Spirit of glory—indeed, the Spirit of God—rests on me.
If you are mocked because of Christ's name, you are blessed, for the Spirit of glory—indeed, the Spirit of God—rests on you. (I Peter 4:14 CEB)

If I suffer for what is right, I am blessed. I don't fear their threats and do not feel frightened.
But even if you should suffer for what is right, you are blessed. "Do not fear their threats; do not be frightened." (I Peter 3:14 NIV)

Praise

I praise you, God, in your sanctuary; praise you in your mighty heaven! Praise you for your mighty works; praise your unequaled greatness! Praise you with a blast of the ram's horn; praise you with the lyre and harp! Praise you with the tambourine and dancing; praise you with strings and flutes! Praise you with a clash of cymbals; praise you with loud clanging cymbals. Let everything that breathes sing praises to you, Lord! Praise the Lord!
Praise the Lord! Praise God in his sanctuary; praise him in his mighty heaven! Praise him for his mighty works; praise his unequaled greatness! Praise him with a blast of the ram's horn; praise him with the lyre and harp! Praise him with the tambourine and dancing; praise him with strings and flutes! Praise him with a clash of cymbals; praise him with loud clanging cymbals. Let everything that breathes sing praises to the Lord! Praise the Lord! (Psalm 150 NLT)

Our Lord and Ruler, your name is wonderful everywhere on earth! You let your glory be seen in the heavens above.
Our Lord and Ruler, your name is wonderful everywhere on earth! You let your glory be seen in the heavens above. (Psalm 8:1 CEV)

Through you, Jesus, I continually offer to God a sacrifice of praise—the fruit of my lips that openly profess his name.
Through Jesus, therefore, let us continually offer to God a sacrifice of praise—the fruit of lips that openly profess his name. (Hebrews 13:15 NIV)

Praise you, for it is good to sing praises to God; it is pleasant and my praise is beautiful.

Praise the Lord! For it is good to sing praises to our God; for it is pleasant, and praise is beautiful. (Psalm 147:1 NKJV)

You are letting me praise your great and awesome name, for you are holy.
Let them praise Your great and awesome name...He is holy. (Psalm 99:3 NKJV)

I shout joyfully to you, Lord, breaking forth in song, rejoicing and singing your praises.
Shout joyfully to the Lord, all the earth; break forth in song, rejoice, and sing praises. (Psalm 98:4 NKJV)

Thanks be to you, God, who gives me the victory through the Lord Jesus Christ.
But thanks be to God, who gives us the victory through our Lord Jesus Christ. (I Corinthians 15:57 NKJV)

My mouth will tell of your righteous deeds, of your saving acts all day long—though I don't know how to relate them all.
My mouth will tell of your righteous deeds, of your saving acts all day long—though I know not how to relate them all. (Psalm 71:15 NIV)

I honor your wonderful name and worship you, O Lord, the One who is most holy and gracious.
Honor the wonderful name of the Lord, and worship the Lord most holy and glorious. (Psalm 29:2 CEV)

O Lord, I praise you and kneel down to worship you, the God of Holiness.
Our Lord and our God, we praise you and kneel down to worship you, the God of holiness! (Psalm 99:5 CEV)

Protection/Safety

But as for me, I sing about your power. Each morning I sing with joy about your unfailing love. For you are my refuge, a place of safety when I am in distress.
But as for me, I will sing about your power. Each morning I will sing with joy about your unfailing love. For you have been my refuge, a place of safety when I am in distress. (Psalm 59:16 NLT)

From the ends of the earth, I cry to you for help when my heart is overwhelmed. Thank you for leading me to the towering rock of safety, for you are my safe refuge, a fortress where my enemies cannot reach me. You let me live forever in your sanctuary, safe beneath the shelter of your wings!
From the ends of the earth, I cry to you for help when my heart is overwhelmed. Lead me to the towering rock of safety, for you are my safe refuge, a fortress where my enemies cannot reach me. Let me live forever in your sanctuary, safe beneath the shelter of your wings! (Psalm 61:2-5 NLT)

Thank you, God, for not letting my foot slip. You are my protector, and you won't fall asleep on the job.
God won't let your foot slip. Your protector won't fall asleep on the job. (Psalm 121:3 CEB)

You are the rock where I am safe. You are my shield, my powerful weapon, and my place of shelter. You rescue me and keep me from being hurt. I praise you, Lord! I pray to you, and you rescue me from my enemies.
You are the rock where I am safe. You are my shield, my powerful weapon, and my place of shelter. You rescue me and keep me from being hurt. I praise you, our Lord! I

prayed to you, and you rescued me from my enemies. (2 Samuel 22:3, 4 CEV)

Thank you, Lord, for being my light and my salvation. I don't fear anyone, for you are my fortress, protecting my life.
The Lord is my light and my salvation. Should I fear anyone? The Lord is a fortress protecting my life. (Psalm 27:1 CEB)

Because I live in the shelter of the Most High, I find rest in the shadow of the Almighty. This I declare about you, Lord: You alone are my refuge, my place of safety; you are my God, and I trust you. For you are rescuing me from every trap and protecting me from deadly disease. You are covering me with your feathers and sheltering me with your wings. Your faithful promises are my armor and protection.
I am not afraid of the terrors of the night, nor the arrow that flies in the day. I do not dread the disease that stalks in darkness, nor the disaster that strikes at midday.
Though a thousand fall at my side, though ten thousand are dying around me, these evils will not touch me. I open my eyes, and see how the wicked are punished.
Since I make you, Lord, my refuge and make the Most High my shelter, no evil is conquering me; no plague is coming near my home. For you order your angels to protect me wherever I go. They hold me up with their hands so I won't even hurt my foot on a stone. I trample upon lions and cobras; I crush fierce lions and serpents under my feet!
You rescue me because I love you. You protect me because I trust in your name. When I call on you, you answer; you are with me in trouble. You rescue and honor me. You are rewarding me with a long life and giving me your salvation.

Those who live in the shelter of the Most High will find rest in the shadow of the Almighty. This I declare about the Lord: He alone is my refuge, my place of safety; he is my God, and I trust him. For he will rescue you from every trap and protect you from deadly disease. He will cover you with his feathers. He will shelter you with his wings. His faithful promises are your armor and protection. Do not be afraid of the terrors of the night, nor the arrow that flies in the day. Do not dread the disease that stalks in darkness, nor the disaster that strikes at midday. Though a thousand fall at your side, though ten thousand are dying around you, these evils will not touch you. Just open your eyes, and see how the wicked are punished. If you make the Lord your refuge, if you make the Most High your shelter, no evil will conquer you; no plague will come near your home. For he will order his angels to protect you wherever you go. They will hold you up with their hands so you won't even hurt your foot on a stone. You will trample upon lions and cobras; you will crush fierce lions and serpents under your feet! The Lord says, "I will rescue those who love me. I will protect those who trust in my name.When they call on me, I will answer; I will be with them in trouble. I will rescue and honor them. I will reward them with a long life and give them my salvation." (Psalm 91 NLT)

Thank you that I do not fear bad news but confidently trust you to care for me.
They do not fear bad news; they confidently trust the Lord to care for them. (Psalm 112:7 NLT)

Because I listen to Wisdom, I live securely, in confident trust, without fear or dread of evil.
But whoso hearkens to me [Wisdom] shall dwell securely and in confident trust and shall be quiet, without fear or dread of evil. (Proverbs 1:33 AMP)

Provision

Thank you, God, for liberally supplying all my needs according to your riches in glory in Christ Jesus.
And my God will liberally supply (fill to the full) your every need according to His riches in glory in Christ Jesus. (Philippians 4:19 AMP)

Thank you that because I bring my tithe, you are now throwing open the floodgates of heaven and pouring out so much blessing that there is not room enough to store it.
Bring the whole tithe into the storehouse, that there may be food in my house. Test me in this," says the Lord Almighty, "and see if I will not throw open the floodgates of heaven and pour out so much blessing that there will not be room enough to store it. (Malachi 3:10 NIV)

You, God, have never forsaken me, and my children have plenty of food. I am generous and lend freely to others; my children are a blessing.
I was young and now I am old, yet I have never seen the righteous forsaken or their children begging bread. They are always generous and lend freely; their children will be a blessing. (Psalm 37:25, 26 NIV)

Thank you that because I have given generously to others, I am receiving in full a gift that is running over and poured back into my lap.
Give, and you will receive. Your gift will return to you in full—pressed down, shaken together to make room for more, running over, and poured into your lap. The amount you give will determine the amount you get back. (Luke 6:38 NLT)

Thank you for showing me your approval and making my efforts successful.
And may the Lord our God show us his approval and make our efforts successful. Yes, make our efforts successful! (Psalm 90:17 NLT)

Thank you for commanding a blessing to be with me in all the work I do in the land you are giving me.
The Lord will command the blessing to be with you—in your barns and on all the work you do—and he will bless you on the land the Lord your God is giving you. (Deuteronomy 28:8 CEB)

You are guiding me continually and satisfying my soul in drought. I am like a spring of water, whose waters do not fail.
The Lord will guide you continually, and satisfy your soul in drought, and strengthen your bones; you shall be like a watered garden, and like a spring of water, whose waters do not fail. (Isaiah 58:11 NKJV)

I am truly happy because I am kind to the poor, and now you, Lord, are rescuing me when I am in trouble.
Those who pay close attention to the poor are truly happy! The Lord rescues them during troubling times. (Psalm 41:1 CEB)

Thank you for making me successful in everything I do. I have plenty of money to lend to others, but I won't need to borrow any myself.
He will make you successful in everything you do. You will have plenty of money to lend to other nations, but you won't need to borrow any yourself. (Deuteronomy 28:12b CEV)

Purity

Thank you that I am running from anything that stimulates youthful lusts. Instead, I now pursue righteous living, faithfulness, love and peace, enjoying the companionship of those who call on you with pure hearts.
Run from anything that stimulates youthful lusts. Instead, pursue righteous living, faithfulness, love, and peace. Enjoy the companionship of those who call on the Lord with pure hearts. (2 Timothy 2:22 NLT)

I am careful to live a blameless life and lead a life of integrity in my own home. I refuse to look at anything vile and vulgar. I reject perverse ideas and stay away from every evil.
I will be careful to live a blameless life—when will you come to help me? I will lead a life of integrity in my own home. I will refuse to look at anything vile and vulgar. I hate all who deal crookedly; I will have nothing to do with them. I will reject perverse ideas and stay away from every evil. (Psalm 101:2-4 NLT)

I am staying pure by obeying your word.
How can a young person stay pure? By obeying your word. (Psalm 119:9 NLT)

Thank you that I am not controlled by my body, but am killing every desire for the wrong kind of sex. You are helping me to not be immoral, indecent or have evil thoughts. Neither am I greedy, which is the same as worshipping idols.
Don't be controlled by your body. Kill every desire for the wrong kind of sex. Don't be immoral or indecent or have evil thoughts. Don't be greedy, which is the same as worshiping idols. (Colossians 3:5 The Voice)

Thank you that I am abstaining from fleshly lusts which war against my soul. Instead, I am conducting myself honorably among people, and my good works, which they observe, glorify you, God.

Beloved, I beg you as sojourners and pilgrims, abstain from fleshly lusts which war against the soul, having your conduct honorable among the Gentiles, that when they speak against you as evildoers, they may, by your good works which they observe, glorify God in the day of visitation. (I Peter 2:11-12 NKJV)

I am obeying my father's commands, and not neglecting my mother's instruction. When I walk, their counsel leads me. When I sleep, they protect me. When I wake up, they advise me. For their command is a lamp and their instruction a light; their corrective discipline is the way to life. It keeps me from the immoral woman, from the smooth tongue of a promiscuous woman.

My son, obey your father's commands, and don't neglect your mother's instruction. When you walk, their counsel will lead you. When you sleep, they will protect you. When you wake up, they will advise you. For their command is a lamp and their instruction a light; their corrective discipline is the way to life. It will keep you from the immoral woman, from the smooth tongue of a promiscuous woman. (Proverbs 6:20, 22-24 NLT)

Thank you that I am running from immoral behavior.
Run from immoral behavior. (I Corinthians 6:18a The Voice)

Revival

Restore us, Lord God Almighty; make your face shine on us, that we may be saved.
Restore us, Lord God Almighty; make your face shine on us, that we may be saved. (Psalm 80:19 NIV)

All the ends of the earth remember and turn to you, Lord, and all the families of the nations are now bowing down and worshiping before you.
All the ends of the earth shall remember and turn to the Lord, and all the families of the nations shall bow down and worship before You. (Psalm 22:27 AMP)

More and more believers in you, Lord, are being added to our church.
Indeed, more and more believers in the Lord, large numbers of both men and women, were added to the church. (Acts 5:14 CEB)

We are seeking you, Lord, while you can still be found; we call while you are yet near. The wicked are abandoning their ways and the sinful their schemes. They are returning to you so that you may have mercy on them because you are generous with forgiveness.
Seek the Lord when he can still be found; call him while he is yet near. Let the wicked abandon their ways and the sinful their schemes. Let them return to the Lord so that he may have mercy on them, to our God, because he is generous with forgiveness. (Isaiah 55:6, 7 CEB)

We are not delaying, but are being baptized; and by calling upon your name, our sins are being washed away.

And now, why do you delay? Rise and be baptized, and by calling upon His name, wash away your sins. (Acts 22:16 AMP)

Thank you that our church is growing daily because people are being saved.
And the Lord added to the church daily those who were being saved. (Acts 2:47b NKJV)

Thank you that your powerful presence is with us, so a great number of people are learning to believe. They are trusting in you and have turned and surrendered themselves to you.
And the presence of the Lord was with them with power, so that a great number [learned] to believe (to adhere to and trust in and rely on the Lord) and turned and surrendered themselves to Him. (Acts 11:21 AMP)

Thank you that your word has spread and the number of disciples is multiplying greatly.
Then the word of God spread, and the number of the disciples multiplied greatly in Jerusalem, and a great many of the priests were obedient to the faith. (Acts 6:7 NKJV)

Spiritual Growth

Thank you for producing this kind of fruit in my life: love, joy, peace, patience, kindness, goodness, faithfulness, gentleness and self-control. But the Holy Spirit produces this kind of fruit in our lives: love, joy, peace, patience, kindness, goodness, faithfulness, gentleness, and self-control. There is no law against these things! (Galatians 5:22, 23 NLT)

I thank you, glorious Father, for giving me the Spirit of wisdom and revelation so that I know you better. The eyes of my heart are being enlightened so that I know the hope to which you have called me, the riches of your glorious inheritance in your holy people, and your incomparably great power for me because I believe. I keep asking that the God of our Lord Jesus Christ, the glorious Father, may give you the Spirit of wisdom and revelation, so that you may know him better. I pray that the eyes of your heart may be enlightened in order that you may know the hope to which he has called you, the riches of his glorious inheritance in his holy people, and his incomparably great power for us who believe. (Ephesians 1:17-19a NIV)

From your glorious, unlimited resources you are empowering me with inner strength through your Spirit. You are making your home in my heart as I trust in you. My roots are growing down into your love and keeping me strong. I have the power to understand, as all God's people should, how wide, how long, how high, and how deep your love is and am experiencing the love of Christ, though it is too great to understand fully. Thus I am being made complete with all the fullness of life and power that comes from you.

I pray that from his glorious, unlimited resources he will empower you with inner strength through his Spirit. Then Christ will make his home in your hearts as you trust in him. Your roots will grow down into God's love and keep you strong. And may you have the power to understand, as all God's people should, how wide, how long, how high, and how deep his love is. May you experience the love of Christ, though it is too great to understand fully. Then you will be made complete with all the fullness of life and power that comes from God. (Ephesians 3:16-19 NLT)

You are answering my prayer: that my love is becoming even more and more rich with knowledge and all kinds of insight. Now I am able to decide what really matters and be sincere and blameless on the day of Christ. I am being filled with the fruit of righteousness, which comes from Jesus Christ, in order to give glory and praise to you.
This is my prayer: that your love might become even more and more rich with knowledge and all kinds of insight. I pray this so that you will be able to decide what really matters and so you will be sincere and blameless on the day of Christ. I pray that you will then be filled with the fruit of righteousness, which comes from Jesus Christ, in order to give glory and praise to God. (Philippians 1:9-11 CEB)

Thank you, God, for giving me complete knowledge of your will as well as spiritual wisdom and understanding. The way I live always honors and pleases you, and my life produces every kind of good fruit. All the while, I am growing as I learn to know you better and better. You are strengthening me with all your glorious power so I have all the endurance and patience I need. I am being filled with joy, always thanking you, Father. You have enabled me to share in the inheritance that belongs to your people, who live in the light.

We ask God to give you complete knowledge of his will and to give you spiritual wisdom and understanding. Then the way you live will always honor and please the Lord, and your lives will produce every kind of good fruit. All the while, you will grow as you learn to know God better and better. We also pray that you will be strengthened with all his glorious power so you will have all the endurance and patience you need. May you be filled with joy, always thanking the Father. He has enabled you to share in the inheritance that belongs to his people, who live in the light. (Colossians 1:9b-12 NLT)

I consider it pure joy whenever I face trials of many kinds, because I know that the testing of my faith produces perseverance.
Consider it pure joy, my brothers and sisters, whenever you face trials of many kinds, because you know that the testing of your faith produces perseverance. (James 1:2, 3 NIV)

I am guarding my heart above all else, for everything I do flows from it.
Above all else, guard your heart, for everything you do flows from it. (Proverbs 4:23 NIV)

Trust/Faith

Thank you that because I trust in you I am not being disgraced.
As the Scriptures tell us, "Anyone who trusts in him will never be disgraced. (Romans 10:11 NLT)

I am trusting in you with all my heart and not leaning on my own understanding; I am submitting all my ways to you, and you are directing my paths.
Trust in the Lord with all your heart and lean not on your own understanding; in all your ways submit to him, and he will make your paths straight. (Proverbs 3:5, 6 NIV)

Whenever I'm afraid, I put my trust in you. I trust in God and won't be afraid. What can mere flesh do to me?
Whenever I'm afraid, I put my trust in you—in God, whose word I praise. I trust in God; I won't be afraid. What can mere flesh do to me? (Psalm 56:3, 4 CEB)

Because I hope in you, I will not be disappointed.
Those who hope in me will not be disappointed. (Isaiah 49:23b NIV)

My faith doesn't depend on people's wisdom but on your power, God.
I did this so that your faith might not depend on the wisdom of people but on the power of God. (I Corinthians 2:5 CEB)

I am trusting you, O Lord, saying, "You are my God!" My future is in your hands.
But I am trusting you, O Lord, saying, "You are my God!" My future is in your hands. (Psalm 31:14, 15b NLT)

I believe that you are now hearing and answering my prayers.
Therefore I tell you, whatever you ask for in prayer, believe that you have received it, and it will be yours. (Mark 11:24 NIV)

Nothing is impossible for you, God.
Nothing is impossible for God. (Luke 1:37 CEB)

I put all my hope in you, and you have leaned down to me, listening to my cry for help.
I put all my hope in the Lord. He leaned down to me; he listened to my cry for help. (Psalm 40:1 CEB)

I am living by faith.
For in it the righteousness of God is revealed from faith to faith; as it is written, "The just shall live by faith." (Romans 1:17 NKJV)

My faith is coming from hearing the Good News about you, Christ.
So faith comes from hearing, that is, hearing the Good News about Christ. (Romans 10:17 NLT)

Wife

My husband trusts me, and I am greatly enriching his life. I bring him good, not harm, as long as I am alive.
Her husband can trust her, and she will greatly enrich his life. She brings him good, not harm, all the days of her life. (Proverbs 31:11, 12 NLT)

My husband and I are submitting to one another out of reverence for you, Christ.
And further, submit to one another out of reverence for Christ. (Ephesians 5:21 NLT)

When I speak, my words are wise, and I always give instructions with kindness.
When she speaks, her words are wise, and she gives instructions with kindness. (Proverbs 31:26 NLT)

I look out for how things are going in my household and do not eat the bread of idleness, gossip, discontent or self-pity.
She looks well to how things go in her household, and the bread of idleness (gossip, discontent, and self-pity) she will not eat. (Proverbs 31:27 AMP)

Thank you that I am submitting to my husband as I do to you, Lord.
Wives, submit yourselves to your own husbands as you do to the Lord. (Ephesians 5:22 NIV)

I am submitting to my husband so that even though he doesn't believe the Good News, he is being won over, not by my words, but by my pure and reverent life.
Wives, in the same way submit yourselves to your own husbands so that, if any of them do not believe the word,

they may be won over without words by the behavior of their wives, when they see the purity and reverence of your lives. (I Peter 3:1, 2 NIV)

Thank you that my husband is rejoicing in me, the wife of his youth.
Rejoice in the wife of your youth. (Proverbs 5:18b CEB)

You are helping me to respect and reverence my husband. I notice, regard, honor, prefer, revere, and esteem him; and I defer to him, praise him, and love and admire him exceedingly.
And let the wife see that she respects and reverences her husband [that she notices him, regards him, honors him, prefers him, venerates, and esteems him; and that she defers to him, praises him, and loves and admires him exceedingly]. (Ephesians 5:33b AMP)

We love each other with love that is from you, God.
Beloved, let us love one another, for love is of God; and everyone who loves is born of God and knows God. (I John 4:7 NKJV)

Wisdom

I am asking you for wisdom, and I thank you for giving it to me; you are not rebuking me for asking.
If you need wisdom, ask our generous God, and he will give it to you. He will not rebuke you for asking. (James 1:5 NLT)

Thank you that rather than always thinking my way is right, I listen to advice.
Fools see their own way as right, but the wise listen to advice. (Proverbs 12:15 CEB)

I am careful to live my life wisely, taking advantage of every opportunity because these are evil times. Instead of being ignorant, I understand your will, Lord.
So be careful to live your life wisely, not foolishly. Take advantage of every opportunity because these are evil times. Because of this, don't be ignorant, but understand the Lord's will. (Ephesians 5:15-17 CEB)

Thank you for giving me your wisdom, which is pure, peace-loving, considerate, submissive, full of mercy and good fruit, impartial and sincere.
But the wisdom that comes from heaven is first of all pure; then peace-loving, considerate, submissive, full of mercy and good fruit, impartial and sincere. (James 3:17 NIV)

I am showing wisdom by not talking too much and displaying understanding by being even-tempered.
The one who has knowledge uses words with restraint, and whoever has understanding is even-tempered. (Proverbs 17:27 NIV)

Thank you that I am getting all the advice and instruction I can, so I will be wise the rest of my life.

Get all the advice and instruction you can, so you will be wise the rest of your life. (Proverbs 19:20 NLT)

I am committing myself to getting instruction and listening carefully to words of knowledge.

Commit yourself to instruction; listen carefully to words of knowledge. (Proverbs 23:12 NLT)

Because I fear you, I am gaining wisdom; knowledge of the Holy One is resulting in understanding.

The fear of the Lord is the beginning of wisdom, and knowledge of the Holy One is understanding. (Proverbs 9:10 NIV)

Witnessing

I am following you, and you are teaching me how to fish for people.
"Come, follow me," he said, "and I'll show you how to fish for people." (Matthew 4:19 CEB)

I am going into all the world and preaching the gospel to everyone.
And He said to them, "Go into all the world and preach the gospel to every creature." (Mark 6:15 NKJV)

Thank you that I am always prepared to give an answer to everyone who asks the reason for my hope. I do this with gentleness and respect.
Always be prepared to give an answer to everyone who asks you to give the reason for the hope that you have. But do this with gentleness and respect. (I Peter 3:15 NIV)

I am now going and making disciples of all nations, baptizing them in the name of the Father, Son and Holy Spirit, and teaching them to observe all the things you have commanded. And you are with me always, even to the end of the age.
Go therefore and make disciples of all the nations, baptizing them in the name of the Father and of the Son and of the Holy Spirit, teaching them to observe all things that I have commanded you; and lo, I am with you always, even to the end of the age. (Matthew 28:19, 20 NKJV)

Thank you that I am preaching boldly about you, Lord, and you are proving this message through miraculous signs and wonders.
But the apostles stayed there a long time, preaching boldly about the grace of the Lord. And the Lord proved their

message was true by giving them power to do miraculous signs and wonders. (Acts 14:3 NLT)

Thank you that I am not ashamed to proclaim the gospel of Christ, for it is the power of God, saving everyone who believes.
For I am not ashamed of the gospel of Christ, for it is the power of God to salvation for everyone who believes, for the Jew first and also for the Greek. (Romans 1:16 NKJV)

I am receiving power since the Holy Spirit has come upon me, and I am your witness here in my hometown and throughout the rest of the earth.
Rather, you will receive power when the Holy Spirit has come upon you, and you will be my witnesses in Jerusalem, in all Judea and Samaria, and to the end of the earth. (Acts 1:8 CEB)

Thank you that my light is shining before others so that they may see my good deeds and glorify you, Father.
In the same way, let your light shine before others, that they may see your good deeds and glorify your Father in heaven. (Matthew 5:16 NIV)

Thanks be to you, who always leads me in triumph and through me spreads everywhere the fragrance of the knowledge of God.
But thanks be to God, Who in Christ always leads us in triumph [as trophies of Christ's victory] and through us spreads and makes evident the fragrance of the knowledge of God everywhere. (2 Corinthians 2:14 AMP)

I am the light of the world and am letting that light shine everywhere I go so men and women may see my good actions and my devotion to you. Because of this, they are turning and praising you, my Father in heaven.

And you, beloved, are the light of the world...Let your light shine everywhere you go, that you may illumine creation, so men and women everywhere may see your good actions, may see creation at its fullest, may see your devotion to Me, and may turn and praise your Father in heaven because of it. (Matthew 5:14, 16 The Voice)

I cried as I went out to plant seeds but now am celebrating as I bring in the crops.
I cried as I went out to plant seeds, but now am celebrating as I bring in the crops. (Psalm 126:5 CEV)

Thank you that as I share my faith with others, they come to know all the blessings you have given us.
As you share your faith with others, I pray that they may come to know all the blessings Christ has given us. (Philemon 6 CEV)

You are now helping me to go out and tell everyone I meet to come to you.
Go out to the street corners and tell everyone you meet to come to the banquet. (Matthew 22:9 CEV)

You have set me free; now I am telling the world how you freed me from oppression.
All of you set free by God, tell the world! Tell how he freed you from oppression. (Psalm 107:2 The Message)

Thank you for helping me to open their eyes so they are turning from darkness to light and from the power of Satan to God. Now their sins are forgiven, and by faith in you, they are becoming part of your holy people.
I want you to open their eyes, so that they will turn from darkness to light and from the power of Satan to God. Then their sins will be forgiven, and by faith in me they will become part of God's holy people. (Acts 26:18 CEV)

Women

Rather than focusing on outward beauty, I am adorned with inner beauty that comes from a gentle and quiet spirit.
Your beauty should not come from outward adornment, such as elaborate hairstyles and the wearing of gold jewelry or fine clothes. Rather, it should be that of your inner self, the unfading beauty of a gentle and quiet spirit, which is of great worth in God's sight. (I Peter 3:3, 4 NIV)

I am clothed with strength and dignity and laugh without fear of the future.
She is clothed with strength and dignity, and she laughs without fear of the future. (Proverbs 31:25 NLT)

Because I fear you, I am praised.
Charm is deceitful and beauty is passing, but a woman who fears the Lord, she shall be praised. (Proverbs 31:30 NKJV)

Thank you that the light in my eyes brings joy to others' hearts, and my good news brings health to their bones.
Light in a messenger's eyes brings joy to the heart, and good news gives health to the bones. (Proverbs 15:30 AMP)

Thank you that I have the mind of Christ.
But we have the mind of Christ. (I Corinthians 2:16b)

I always rejoice in you, Lord, delighting in you.
Rejoice in the Lord always [delight, gladden yourselves in Him]; again I say, Rejoice! (Philippians 4:4 AMP)

You have taught me since I was young, and now I declare your marvelous deeds.

Since my youth, God, you have taught me, and to this day I declare your marvelous deeds. (Proverbs 71:17 NIV)

Thank you that I receive respect because I am gracious.
A gracious woman will be respected (Proverbs 11:16a CEV)

I open my hand to the poor and reach out to help the needy, whether in body, mind, or spirit.
She opens her hand to the poor, yes, she reaches out her filled hands to the needy [whether in body, mind, or spirit]. (Proverbs 31:20 AMP)

I rejoice because I put my trust in you and shout for joy because you defend me. Because I love your name, I am joyful in you.
But let all those rejoice who put their trust in You; let them ever shout for joy, because You defend them; let those also who love Your name be joyful in You. (Psalm 5:11 NKJV)

Thank you that I am beautiful on the inside, with a gentle, peaceful spirit. This type of beauty is very precious in your sight.
Instead, make yourselves beautiful on the inside, in your hearts, with the enduring quality of a gentle, peaceful spirit. This type of beauty is very precious in God's eyes. (I Peter 3:4 CEB)

Thank you that I am full of good courage, and you have strengthened my heart; my hope is in you.
Be of good courage, and He shall strengthen your heart, all you who hope in the Lord. (Psalm 31:24 NKJV)

Words/Mouth

You, God, have tested my thoughts and examined my heart in the night. You have scrutinized me and found nothing wrong. I am determined not to sin in what I say.
You have tested my thoughts and examined my heart in the night. You have scrutinized me and found nothing wrong. I am determined not to sin in what I say. (Psalm 17:3 NLT)

The words you are giving me are always gracious.
Words from the mouth of the wise are gracious, but fools are consumed by their own lips. (Ecclesiastes 10:12 NIV)

I am being careful in what I say because I know I will have to answer on Judgment Day for every useless word I speak. Because my words please you, I will be judged innocent rather than condemned as guilty.
I tell you that people will have to answer on Judgment Day for every useless word they speak. By your words you will be either judged innocent or condemned as guilty. (Matthew 12:36, 37 CEB)

Instead of using foul or abusive language, everything I say is good and helpful, so that my words are an encouragement to those who hear them.
Don't use foul or abusive language. Let everything you say be good and helpful, so that your words will be an encouragement to those who hear them. (Ephesians 4:29 NLT)

You are helping me speak and teaching me what I should say.
Now go! I'll help you speak, and I'll teach you what you should say. (Exodus 4:12 CEB)

Thank you, Lord, for reaching out your hand and touching my mouth. You have now put your words in my mouth.
Then the Lord reached out his hand and touched my mouth and said to me, "I have put my words in your mouth." (Jeremiah 1:9 NIV)

Because too much talk leads to sin, I am being sensible and keeping my mouth shut.
Too much talk leads to sin. Be sensible and keep your mouth shut. (Proverbs 10:19 NLT)

Thank you that my kind words to others are like honey— sweet to their soul and healthy for their body.
Kind words are like honey—sweet to the soul and healthy for the body. (Proverbs 16:24 NLT)

Thank you that my speech is always gracious and sprinkled with insight so that I know how to respond to every person.
Your speech should always be gracious and sprinkled with insight so that you may know how to respond to every person. (Colossians 4:6 CEB)

Because I guard my mouth and tongue, I keep myself from trouble.
Those who guard their mouths and their tongues guard themselves from trouble. (Proverbs 21:23 CEB)

Thank you that I keep my tongue from evil and my lips from speaking lies.
Then you must keep your tongue from evil and keep your lips from speaking lies! (Psalm 34:13 CEB)

Work

I am working willingly at whatever I do, as though I am working for you, Lord, rather than for people.
Work willingly at whatever you do, as though you were working for the Lord rather than for people. (Colossians 3:23 NLT)

Because I am committing my work to you, my plans are succeeding.
Commit your work to the Lord, and your plans will succeed. (Proverbs 16:3 CEB)

This is your gift to me, God: I am enjoying the results of all my hard work.
Moreover, this is the gift of God: that all people should eat, drink, and enjoy the results of their hard work. (Ecclesiastes 3:13 CEB)

Thank you that all my hard work is bringing a profit.
All hard work brings a profit, but mere talk leads only to poverty. (Proverbs 14:23 NIV)

The Spirit you have given me is not timid as I do my work, but provides power, love and self-discipline.
For the Spirit God gave us does not make us timid, but gives us power, love and self-discipline. (2 Timothy 1:7 NIV)

I am doing my work with all my might.
Whatever your hand finds to do, do it with your might. (Ecclesiastes 9: 10 NKJV)

You have always put a wall of protection around me and my home and property. You have made me prosper in everything I do.
You have always put a wall of protection around him and his home and his property. You have made him prosper in everything he does. Look how rich he is! (Job 1:10 NLT)

I am doing all of my work for your honor and glory, God.
So then, whether you eat or drink, or whatever you may do, do all for the honor and glory of God. (I Corinthians 10:31 AMP)

Thank you for comforting my heart and establishing me in every good word and work.
...comfort your hearts and establish you in every good word and work. (2 Thessalonians 2:17 NKJV)

Thank you that I do all my work through you who gives me strength.
I can do all this through him who gives me strength. (Philippians 4:13 NIV)

I now do all my work without complaining and arguing, so that no one can criticize me.
Do everything without complaining and arguing, so that no one can criticize you. (Philippians 2:14, 15a NLT)

Thank you that I now work with enthusiasm, as though I am working for you rather than people. You reward me for the good I do.
Work with enthusiasm, as though you were working for the Lord rather than for people. Remember that the Lord will reward each one of us for the good we do, whether we are slaves or free. (Ephesians 6:7, 8 NLT)